WINNING STRATEGIES FOR DIABETES

WHO SAYS YOU CAN'T LOWER BLOOD SUGAR TO NORMAL AND LIVE HEALTHIER?

DAVID F. WILSON

ANIVYA PUBLISHING

DISCLAIMER

The author has made every attempt to be as accurate and complete as possible in the creation of this publication/PDF, however he / she does not warrant or represent at any time that the contents within are accurate, due to the rapidly changing nature of Internet content. The author assumes no responsibility for errors, omissions, or contrary interpretation of the subject matter herein. Any perceived slights of specific persons, peoples, or organizations other published materials are unintentional and used for educational purposes only.

This information is not intended for use as a source of MEDICAL, legal, business, accounting or financial advice. All readers are advised to seek services of competent professionals in the MEDICAL, legal, business, accounting, and finance field. No representation is made or implied that the reader will do as well from using the techniques, strategies, methods, systems, or ideas herein as using any others; rather it is presented for news value only.

The author does not assume any responsibility or liability whatsoever for what you choose to do with this information. Use your own judgment. Consult appropriate professionals before starting a business. Any perceived remark or comment in reference to organizations or people, and any resemblance to characters living, dead or otherwise, real or fictitious, does not mean that they support this content in any way.

There are no guarantees of income to be made, traffic delivered or other promises of any kind. Readers are cautioned to rely on their own judgment about their individual circumstances and to act accordingly. By reading any document, the reader agrees that under no circumstances is the author responsible for any losses, direct or indirect, that are incurred as a result of use of the information contained within this document, including - but not limited to errors, omissions, or inaccuracies.

CONTENTS

Introduction   1

1   What really is diabetes?   5

2   It isn't a 'cure' but it is very close   19

3   Diabetes from another perspective   35

4   Diabetic pre-suppression starter   39

5   Restoring health is a process   59

6   How it all worked for 'Ralph'   69

7   Conclusion and beyond   83

INTRODUCTION

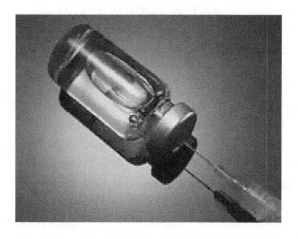

Diabetes. The disease is prolific and more people are contracting it. According to the *American Diabetes Association*, here are some alarming statistics:

- Almost 30 million children and adults in the United States have diabetes.

- 86 million Americans have pre-diabetes.

- 1.4 million Americans are diagnosed with diabetes every year.

- People die on average at least 6 years sooner than those without the disease.

Source:https://professional.diabetes.org/sites/prof essional.diabetes.org/files/media/fast_facts_12-

Does this mean that diabetes is growing out of control? Why is this happening? Here's what *Harvard Health* had to say:

"Diabetes has been on the upswing since the 1960s, fueled largely by Americans' penchant for eating too much and exercising too little. The combination of excess weight and inactivity makes tissues resistant to insulin, which snowballs into diabetes. **The CDC's new warning factors in** the continuing spread of obesity and inactivity with the aging of the U.S. population, the higher risk for diabetes in rapidly growing minority populations, and improvements in medical care that help people with diabetes live longer."

Source:http://www.health.harvard.edu/blog/explo sion-in-diabetes-isnt-inevitable-20101029739

If these alarming facts are of concern to you, just imagine what the world will look like in another 20 years. Diabetes is currently affecting over 371 million people worldwide. If projections hold we could see double the number of people develop diabetes in just the next twenty years alone . . . Yet there is hope for sufferers.

That is what this eBook is all about: hope, change and modern research. There are ways to improve your life as a diabetic, *to finally limit or even fully*

suppress diabetes so as to lessen its impact and destructive force.

Let's take this journey together right now.

WHAT REALLY IS DIABETES?

Diabetes is an often-misunderstood "disease" and is NOT what you may have been told it is. Here is the typical generic description of what diabetes is said to be, to start our discussion:

---

di·a·be·tes
/ˌdīəˈbēdēz, ˌdīəˈbēdis/

noun

> a metabolic disease in which the body's inability to produce any or enough insulin causes elevated levels of glucose in the blood.

As you can see, this is a standard definition, simply explained and it even makes sense. Yet it is NOT what diabetes *really* is. . .

If there was a proper definition, one that had a

solution or potential treatment for the disease, science would have described it this way: "**Diabetes is a form of intoxication (poison) that is the result of toxic overload of your cells which interferes with your body's ability to produce insulin.**" – My quote and it is the BEST definition.

Diabetes is like being poisoned? YES. The term intoxication actually is used to describe poisoning, such as the term *foodborne intoxication*. So, let's take a look at the definition of foodborne intoxication (yes, this will all make sense soon):

"Foodborne infection is caused by the ingestion of food containing live bacteria which grow and establish themselves in the human intestinal tract. **Foodborne intoxication is caused by ingesting food containing toxins** formed by bacteria which resulted from the bacterial growth in the food item."

Source: http://food.unl.edu/food-poisoning-foodborne-illness

What do you notice here? A foodborne illness *results in an intoxication* that affects the entire body, makes you sick and will continue making you sick until the bacteria / toxins leave your body.

I am here to say that **Diabetes is CAUSED by toxins** in your food. Some of those toxins are sugar, but mostly they are contaminants in food, water, air and the myriad of chemicals we are all exposed to daily. These toxins bio – accumulate (which is why we become pre-diabetic first) until your body can no longer regulate blood glucose.

When you eat enough toxic food, your body begins to break down.

When toxins build up in your body, things begin to go wrong. This will destroy the body's ability to self-regulate, especially at a cellular level.

This is because toxins **burn out control receptors in your cells** and over time cause a gradual reduction in the ability to control many hormones in the body, including insulin production and insulin resistance. Modern medicine says there is no cure for diabetes and while that is technically true (medicine does not recognize holistic medicine), there are ways to suppress the disease so much, it has no impact on your life.

WHY THERE IS NO MEDICAL CURE – FOLLOW THE MONEY

Recently I read an article saying scientists are claiming type I diabetes (essentially insulin dependent) is now quite possibly reversible in time:

". . .type 1 diabetes has long been thought to be a permanent condition that requires lifelong insulin dependence. Excitingly, a new study published just last month suggests that a 'fasting mimicking diet" could effectively reverse the pathology of type 1 diabetes in mice."

Source: https://chriskresser.com/could-type-1-diabetes-be-reversible-after-all/

Over the years I have seen hundreds of related studies and information by researchers that indicate the scientific community not only KNOWS diabetes is reversible, but that there are also many "folk cures" that have been completely discounted by our society.

Why is this the case for diabetics? Most people already know the answer:

"If you are a diabetes patient, you are Big Pharma's best friend. **You have been earmarked for the rest of your life as a cash cow** for the companies who make diabetes medicines, syringes, blood sugar monitors, insulin, cotton swabs, and more. But there is a little secret that the pharmaceutical companies don't want you to know."

Source: http://naturalsociety.com/big-pharma-afraid-diabetes-patients-will-find/

The 'secret' is that YOU are capable of eliminating pre-diabetes and type II diabetes all on your own. You can suppress type I diabetes and, in some cases, 'cure' the disease (almost complete suppression) just with over the counter products that are cheap, and that I will share with you -- as well as multiple folk 'cures' that have been used for over a hundred years and seem to work better than pharmaceutical drugs.

According to today's researchers, cures for diabetes have **been hidden from the general public for over 40 years** because as soon as a cure is developed, companies that produce diabetic drugs and supplies will purchase this research / information to keep it quiet:

"There are numerous examples of well-educated, innovative doctors and scientists who have created alternative medical treatments that far supersede conventional drug treatments, and yet they are more frequently than not shunned, persecuted, or even prosecuted for their efforts." - Dr. Mercola

Source:
http://articles.mercola.com/sites/articles/archive/2009/02/14/a-possible-cure-for-diabetes-ignored-by-big-pharma.aspx

Follow the money could not be truer here.

So now you know that big corporations drive commerce by banking on disease maintenance but NOT curatives.

Think about it: why should any corporation making

literally BILLIONS of dollars a year (471 BILLION on average yearly in this market) ever want to find a cure? Drug companies **make customers not cures** and if you are one of the customers, I strongly suggest you take your health strongly in your own hands.

People are waking up to this ongoing scam.

Now the drug companies see that there is blood in the water over this issue so they are finally being compelled to release a cure; even if that 'cure' creates more health issues and with big Pharma, you can bet it will.

A DIABETIC'S DEFINITION OF DIABETES

Remember what I said about the definition of Diabetes? Diabetes is a form of **toxic overload** that affects your pancreas, liver, gallbladder, and kidneys. The organs become so toxic that over time, they malfunction and eventually replicate malfunctioning cells. As these cells propagate (much like cancer) your body begins a slow decline until Diabetes appears.

The lack of properly functioning cells **is at the heart of many diseases** (i.e. Cancer) and if you are diabetic, you have increased likelihood of developing other secondary illnesses and conditions too.

Nice, huh? Believe me I hated this as well. I was so MAD when I discovered that I have been lied to by:

- **My parents** (who did not know diabetes can be reversed).

- **My friends** (who did not know diabetes can be reversed).

- **My College** (who did not know diabetes can be reversed).

- **My health care provider HMO** (diabetes is not reversible according to them)

- **My doctor** (doctors no longer receive training in holistic medicine, just how to prescribe drugs).

- **The hospital** (who did not know diabetes can be reversed).

Are we seeing a trend here? If you look long enough you will find the fingerprints of big Pharma all over the diabetes lies. Now is the time to take back your health and do so in a way that thousands of sufferers have discovered.

IS YOUR FOOD TOXIC? YES . .

Now we can clearly see that all the hype that is directed at diabetics, especially from the medical industry, is not only unwarranted ***but does not*** *take into consideration the highly toxic diet that is being foisted on us* by large corporations who care nothing about our health and only want to sell all of their crappy junk foods.

As a former diabetic, I've been lectured by:

- Dietitians insisting I remain on a low-fat diet with few carbs. This is despite the fact that low-fat diets are now being proven to cause illness and that we NEED more high quality fats to survive.

- My doctor who insisted the solution is more diabetic drugs and maintenance as opposed to any attempt at a "cure."

- Most people in general telling me I need to follow their advice on diet and exercise and stop being lazy, even though a majority of them are pre-diabetic or toxic or both too...

So now we know that despite all the lies we hear about diabetes, that the biggest problem we have is a society *filled with toxins* in our food, air, water, medicine, cosmetics etc.

It is quite possible to be exposed to **thousands of chemicals DAILY** that are laced throughout every aspect of our society that we are exposed to!

These chemicals will make you sick over time and

unfortunately most of us are not aware that we are consuming them every day in one form or another. Currently you must devise a way to avoid **at least** 80% of the toxic foods, chemicals and additives that you are exposed to on a regular basis. This is the only way to reverse the damage that has been done, which will bring us into our next section in the guide.

STOP EATING JUNK FOODS!

Even if you're not aware of it, **diabetes and the complications** that you experience are now factored to be the seventh leading cause of death in the United States and number 6 worldwide:

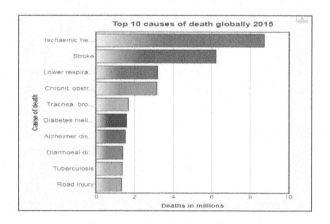

Source:http://www.who.int/mediacentre/factsheets/fs 310/en/

13

What is interesting to note from the chart above is that **every form of death that is experienced**, with the exception of road injury, can be directly or indirectly linked to a junk diet filled with toxin-laden foods!

Diabetes is the seventh leading killer in the United States and number six worldwide, -- you now know this. Those statistics alone are reason enough to invest time and research into also seeing that the majority of related diseases are also part of our studies.

More research is emerging daily that suggests that almost all forms of illness that we experience in a modern society are directly linked to a junk food diet, lack of exercise, lack of proper nutrients and the pressure cooker, super stressful society we all live in.

Can there be any reason *not to see that we are all being poisoned* and many of us are willing participants in our own illnesses? For example, just one "sweetener," aspartame could be one of the worst poisons ever concocted by man, yet it is everywhere in our food chain:

"Aspartame is a neurotoxin. Even ants have sense enough to avoid it. Yet, diet drinks and many foods add this neurotoxin chemical as its sweetener, and they promote it as a heath food to a public that naively puts its trust in the experts. Drink water.

Drink tea. Drink regular soda – anything but the diet sodas. You just might live longer." –Dr. Mercola *Source:* http://aspartame.mercola.com/

It's not just toxins like aspartame in your food that we have to watch out for *but all forms of toxins* that are used to process foods:

"A report by the Union of Concerned Scientists estimates that 70 percent of antibiotics used in this country are given to animals for growth promotion and other non-medical uses. And when all agricultural uses were considered, they estimated the share could be as high as 84 percent! This massive antibiotic overuse is largely responsible for the potent strains of antibiotic-resistant bacteria we are seeing today." –Dr. Mercola

Source:http://articles.mercola.com/sites/articles/archive/2011/05/07/nearly-half-of-us-meat-tainted-with-drugresistant-bacteria.aspx

Perhaps the only way to achieve a completely healthy lifestyle is to make sure all food that passes your lips is wholesome, 100% truly organic and in a form that has not been processed in any way.

Even if you manage to get this type of food, the word 'organic' has changed over the years to just mean most foods grown in the ground. It is also supposed to mean that pesticides and other toxins are not used, but that is not always the case: Have

a read here:
https://www.nal.usda.gov/afsic/organic-productionorganic-food-information-access-tools

HOW ONE MAN REVERSED HIS DIABETES – HIS DOCTOR WAS STUNNED!

I wanted to first give you enough background information on diabetes and the connection to **poor food choices,** and the toxins that they contain, as the main reason why you might be suffering with diabetes.

In addition, you may want to ask me why the heck you should listen to what I have to say. Well that is a good question.

I want to explain to you that I fully understand what you're going through because I have experienced it for many years:

- Often uncontrolled blood glucose readings as high as 400.

- Diabetic secondary conditions like nerve pain.

- Heavy thirst and a need to void often (pee).

- Slow healing ulcers (wounds on the skin) and related pain.

I understand all the things that you're going

16

through, but I want to tell you my story because **it involves a new mindset** in a way that you can take charge of your disease and eventually reverse most, if not all, of the damage and finally gain control over diabetes.

I started out many years ago like most people.

Even though I only ate twice a day I was overweight, unhappy and unhealthy. For many years and couldn't understand why it was difficult to lose weight and I began to notice some diabetic complications.

After visiting my doctor, I was told that I was having issues controlling my blood sugar and that there is a good chance that I was a diabetic and might require insulin.

At the time I knew very little about diabetes and believed all the lies I was told. I was told that I contracted the disease primarily because I consumed large quantities of sugar.

I knew this was untrue.

Yet it wasn't the sugar that I was eating too much of. I had a love of diet Pepsi, which I believe was the reason why I contracted diabetes:

"Research by the Karolinska Institute on 2,800 adults found that those who consumed at least two 200ml servings of soft drinks daily were 2.4 times as likely to suffer from a form of type 2 diabetes."

Source:http://www.telegraph.co.uk/news/2016/10/21/two-diet-drinks-a-day-could-double-the-risk-of-diabetes-study-fi/

Other studies have confirmed that diet soft drinks contain aspartame and/or other types of artificial sweeteners that damage your cells' ability to regulate glucose levels; and new studies show it makes you FAT.

As mentioned earlier, as toxins bio-accumulate in the body, the body begins to break down and cells no longer recognize hormones that control sugar. As more cells become corrupted, the process continues progressively until diseases begin to appear.

It took me about three years of using diabetic medications to come to the realization that my body was not getting better and that the health decreases continued to spiral out of control.

It was at this point that I decided I needed to consider a holistic approach because I had heard of people curing their own diabetes.

IT ISN'T A "CURE" BUT IT IS VERY CLOSE

When I began my initial research into some type of **"folk cure,"** I started by researching diabetes websites, discussion groups, and reading magazines, medical journals, and white papers. I also studied "holistic curatives." Just about anything that was peer reviewed, I would read.

I was particularly interested in what average everyday people were doing to control, suppress or otherwise greatly reduce the effects of diabetes in their life.

I noticed that no doctor that writes prescriptions on a regular basis will agree that diabetes can be "cured" even though research is emerging to the contrary.

Once we understand what the premise of diabetes is, we can begin to see an actual methodology that will suppress the disease with very little work and no impact on your daily life.

Even though doctors will not readily admit that the disease can be 100% cured, **there can be little question that almost any disease under the right conditions in the human body can at least be suppressed** to a point that it can be completely controlled.

Few doctors will argue this point as disease suppression is a wonderful new field of study and it is gaining steam with all diseases.

Your immune system essentially does the same thing every single day; it suppresses disease to a point where it may have little or no effect in your body. Should we be able to do the same thing with diabetes?

No, disease suppression is not a cure, but it is very close . . .

THE REAL TRUTH ABOUT DIABETES AND WHY LIES ARE KILLING YOU

I want to make you aware of a number of myths and half-truths about diabetes. Many of these falsehoods are readily believed today even by some doctors! The truth is, few people actually know what diabetes really is, -- or there would be an accepted cure by big medicine.

Here are the myths that are perpetuating misery and suffering by helping you to maintain your disease:

- ✓ **You cannot eat sugar if you are a diabetic –** yes, you must regulate processed sugar intake but a small amount of sugar, especially from natural sources like locally grown organic honey, are actually quite good for diabetics. Moderation is key and careful timing means an occasional sweet treat will not kill you.

✓ **Type II diabetes is better than type I diabetes -** this myth has been perpetuated for many years. This is based on the premise that not taking insulin means that you are healthier. While physiologically this may be true, people that use insulin can readily regulate their overall blood sugar and keep it lower, thereby reducing the damage that high glucose levels do. Both types of diabetes are considered health risks.

✓ **Type II diabetes only affects fat people -** this is another myth that is untrue. Approximately 30% of people that contract type II diabetes are average weight, and the majority of people that contract type II diabetes are only moderately overweight.

✓ **People with diabetes should eat diabetic food -** nothing could be further from the truth as most types of diabetic foods **are highly processed**. They may not contain much sugar, but as you recall, it is toxic overload that keeps your body from functioning properly and makes you insulin resistant. The best foods for any diabetic to eat are 100% natural and organic whole foods, super foods and a small amount of high quality fats and honey or a pinch of cane sugar (natural) for flavor.

✓ **People with diabetes go blind and lose their legs -** while it is true that people who do not control their glucose level readings can eventually suffer from an amputation or potential blindness, all of this can be prevented by keeping your blood glucose at those levels within the realm of normal (100 - 120 to 140 or at least below 200 whenever possible).

✓ **People with diabetes are more likely to be sick -** this is also completely untrue as long as you maintain a reasonable blood glucose levels. Inflammation based on high glucose readings can lead to secondary infections, which can cause ulcers on your feet, legs etc., so maintain good sugar levels and avoid all of this.

✓ **Diabetes is contagious sometimes -** this is completely false. The only way you can contract diabetes is toxic overload of your body to the point where it can no longer regulate blood glucose levels.

✓ **Diabetics have issues driving cars -** again another crazy myth. The same rules apply to driving like they would to anyone else. As long as you have the ability to see properly and react sufficiently, diabetics are just as skilled as other drivers.

As you can see, there is a whole host of craziness that is actually believed by a majority of people who are unfamiliar with diabetes. If you hear someone repeat any of these myths, please debunk them immediately for the benefit of all of us.

DIABETES TYPE I & II AND WHAT YOU NEED TO KNOW

Some people have a difficult time understanding the difference between type I and type II diabetes. While there are even smaller subset groups (i.e. Gestational diabetes) the real difference is based on the following factors:

- ✓ **Pre-diabetes** - this is when your body is reaching the tipping point between toxic overload and the ability to regulate blood glucose levels. Here your body is having problems processing high levels of glucose in your blood, but the readings are not yet high enough to be called type II diabetes.

- ✓ For example, normal blood glucose readings are approximately 120. Pre-diabetes usually is diagnosed when readings are between 140 -160. Even if your doctor sees elevated readings, you will typically be prescribed a drug like Metformin, which will help regulate and control sugar levels without the need for insulin.

✓ **Type II diabetes** - typically a diagnosis of type II diabetes results when your blood those levels are above 160 and cannot be controlled very easily through diet and exercise. Although type II diabetics are not insulin-dependent, as their pancreas is still producing some insulin, it is not in sufficient amounts. Eventually your pancreas may stop producing insulin altogether, especially if you use prescriptions.

✓ **Type I diabetes** – in this scenario type I diabetics require regular insulin shots in order to replace insulin that is not being produced by the pancreas. Continued use of insulin practically guarantees that your pancreas will never function properly because you're introducing the required insulin into the bloodstream, which prevents the restart of the pancreas.

Regardless of the actual diagnosis that you receive, dealing with both type I and type II diabetes should essentially be the same:

✓ Reduce all intake of processed junk foods and processed sugars.

✓ Stop drinking coffee, alcohol and sports

drinks!

- ✓ Start eating only 100% organic foods that are unprocessed and have not been with any form of pesticides or contaminants.

- ✓ Begin detoxification of your entire body as explained in this guide later on.

- ✓ CONSULT WITH DOCTOR - gradually reduce your diabetic medications as your body regains its health, but always keep your blood glucose levels as close to normal as possible.

- ✓ Drink the cleanest water you can find - typically this is water you may need to manufacture by using proper water filtration. The water that you drink should be 100% toxin free, so find the very best water filter that removes fluorides, glyphosates, and other of dangerous and poisonous toxins. Do not drink municipal city water, do not drink bottled water, rather manufacture your own. I highly suggest looking into <u>a Berkey water filter</u> as this is one of the best water filters you can purchase.

I cannot emphasize enough how drinking **clean water** is absolutely essential to detoxification and recovery from most of the side effects of diabetes.

Don't purchase water from the grocery store, don't buy bottled water because almost all bottled water that is sold is highly contaminated with fluoride and other minerals and toxins that are made to improve the taste, but are also highly toxic.

The goal is to completely detoxify your body so that it can recover and begin functioning normally.

MEDICAL KNOWLEDGE ABOUT DIABETES

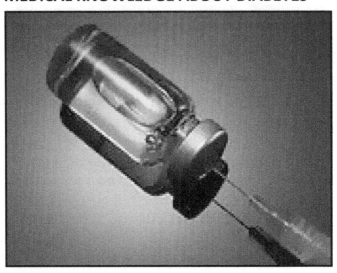

Diabetes is a very serious medical condition that requires daily observation of blood glucose levels and then reacting to those levels by either reducing caloric intake and/or taking medications.

The medical approach to diabetes is not to try to "cure" it but rather manage the disease so that it doesn't kill you.

One of the best ways to prevent health issues from occurring is to first learn how to control your blood sugar. Controlling your blood sugar need not be overly difficult, but you must understand that proper control requires several things:

- ✓ **An understanding** of how certain foods affect your current blood glucose levels.

- ✓ **How to control your glucose levels** by moderating the food you eat and when you eat it.

- ✓ **Constantly monitoring blood glucose levels** and adjusting your medication use contingent on a sliding scale via medications you can use to counter rising sugar levels.

As most diabetics can tell you, they begin to learn exactly what happens after they consume certain foods.

For example, Joe starts out his day with a blood glucose reading of 160. Joe decides he is hungry and would still like to have breakfast so he has two eggs, two strips of bacon and one slice of toast.

An hour after Joe eats, his blood sugar rises to 256. Joe is insulin-dependent so he shoots approximately 6 units of insulin based on a sliding scale of how much he needs. An additional hour later, Joe's reading is 196, not fantastic but below 200. The next day, Joe skips the toast with breakfast and adds 12 ounces of green tea that is unsweetened.

Joe now knows exactly how to achieve a blood glucose rating of lower than 200 just by observing the food that he eats and the amounts. Joe has now "dialed in" breakfast and in the future, he knows exactly what to do to keep his blood sugar below 200.

This is the kind of information that you should **jot down in a daily journal** because the more you understand how your body reacts to certain amounts of food, the easier it will be to maintain those levels.

As you discover the right amounts of food to eat, you can begin structuring your meals so that it will be much easier to maintain proper sugar levels.

Notice that when Joe begins to add to the organic components (i.e. green tea) that his numbers begin to improve almost immediately. Eating whole foods and consuming natural teas is a great start and can be used to add more nutrients to your diet. Almost all diabetics benefit from a completely organic diet with high levels of organic teas.

MANAGE YOUR DIABETES

Since we are discussing the medical model, yes it is possible to manage your diabetes until such time as you are completely detoxified. Below are the steps that most people go through before they realize it is just managing their diabetes. I wanted to present this because the medical model does work to manage diabetes and this is the first step to controlling and eventually suppressing the disease:

✓ **Being diagnosed** - nothing happens in the medical world until you receive a diagnosis. While this bothers some people, being labeled a diabetic is not a death sentence unless you allow it to happen. Getting diagnosed is actually good because now you can quantify exactly what problems you are having and how you can go about correcting them.

✓ **Receiving the final diagnosis** - most doctors will first attempt to discern whether or not you are pre-diabetic. If you happen to be pre-diabetic, there is still hope because you are capable of preventing full-blown diabetes by making some lifestyle changes at this point. Pre-diabetes is fully curable. This is where the false assumption is made that diabetics are simply fat, lazy and sit around all day eating sugar. In reality we now know that toxic overload is the main reason why you are receiving the diagnosis.

✓ **Welcome to the club** - Congratulations! You are now officially a diabetic. Most of us do not want to belong to the club but there are a few perks that we will discuss later.

✓ **Follow your doctor's orders** - It is at this point that your doctor will give you a selection of different medications. I strongly suggest you follow the advice at first while simultaneously following the steps in this guide.

✓ **Start following the steps in this guide.**

DIABETIC RESEARCH DETAILS

Fully understanding the most current research will give you an edge over other people suffering. The latest research also confirms everything I am teaching you here today even if modern medicine does not accept the findings yet.

I want to remind you that a majority of doctors believed less than 100 years ago **that smoking cigarettes as many as possible, was good for your lungs** and help to improve your breathing!

Always remember this example when doctors tell you they know what they're talking about . . .

Still you should follow the advice of your doctor, at least when it comes to managing diabetes. What you should not do is put your entire life in their hands. Use medical knowledge to help you manage the disease and prevent it from getting out of control.

Use the information in this guide to suppress diabetes to the point where it no longer bothers you, causes issues, or makes you ill. Always remember that modern medicine seeks only to maintain or might even worsen your diabetes because there is big money in this disease:

"Mainstream medicine largely fails in treating diabetes – even worsens it – because it refuses to investigate and act on this underlying cause. Insulin sensitivity is key in this matter." –Dr. Mercola
Source: http://www.mercola.com/diabetes.aspx

Holistic practitioners like Doctor Mercola, have been sounding the alarm for many years about diabetes and other diseases that are caused predominantly by lifestyle and the toxins that we consume on a daily basis that eventually damage cells:

"According to the paper titled, "Autoimmunity against a defective ribosomal insulin gene product in type 1 diabetes," the findings "further support the emerging concept that beta cells are destroyed in T1D by a mechanism comparable to classical antitumor responses where the immune system has been trained to survey dysfunctional cells in which errors have accumulated."

Translation in simple laymen's terms: damage to cells causes other cells to attack the bad ones and this "causes" diabetes:

"New study results challenge traditional ideas about the source of type 1 diabetes (T1D). T1D, previously known as juvenile diabetes, affects an estimated 1.5 million Americans and is the result of the loss of insulin-producing cells in the pancreas. The prevailing belief was that the root cause of T1D was the immune system mistakenly identifying those insulin-secreting beta cells as a potential danger and, in turn, destroying them."

Source:www.sciencedaily.com/releases/2017/03/1 70301085412.htm

Yes it is about cell health. With T-cell research also ongoing, replacing damaged T cells is also a viable therapy that can replace insulin:

https://www.theguardian.com/science/2016/dec/08/new-diabetes-treatment-could-eliminate-need-for-insulin-injections

DIABETES FROM ANOTHER PERSPECTIVE

Already you may be looking at diabetes with new eyes. This is because **you finally see diabetes from a different perspective**. You now know that diabetes is a form of toxic overload to the point where your body begins to break down.

Once you know this, you're now ready to begin to explore a different way and/or different perspective on how to deal with diabetes. This will also allow you to analyze information from top experts like Dr. Richard Johnson.

Dr. Richard Johnson is most likely one of the top influential experts when it comes to fully understanding diabetes and its impact on our lives. If you are not aware, Doctor Johnson is known for his award-winning books, *The Sugar Fix* and *The Fat Switch.*

The reason why these books are so important is because they give a new insight when it comes to properly dealing with diabetes from a different perspective:

Insulin resistance - here Dr. Johnson discusses how the rise in use of high fructose corn syrup is one of the top culprits when it comes to insulin resistance.

Weight gain - high fructose corn syrup *is proven* to be the main culprit behind weight gain even if you eat a low volume of overall calories. The toxins direct the body to consume lean body mass as well. This means less muscle, more toxins, in a vicious cycle.

The reason why Dr. Johnson's work is so groundbreaking is because it follows along exactly what we are discussing here. High fructose corn syrup is an additive that is found ubiquitously in food and beverages in our society.

Were you aware that high fructose corn syrup also was processed with a form of mercury (highly toxic and considered a dangerous poison) in small amounts, enough to cause ongoing illnesses, weight gain, metabolic syndrome and a variety of other disorders and diseases?

Here is what Dr. Axe had to say and these were just some of the health issues related to high fructose corn syrup:

➢ Americans consume at least of 50 grams of HFCS every day.

➢ HFCS represents over 40 percent of caloric sweeteners added to foods and beverages.

➢ HFCS can increase the risk of high blood pressure, diabetes and heart disease.

➢ Consumption of HFCS has greatly increased over the years and is a main factor in our current obesity epidemic.

➢ HFCS can cause LGS or leaky gut syndrome.

➢ HFCS contains up to 570 micrograms of health-hazardous mercury per gram.

➢ HFCS has been shown to promote cancer.

➢ The average 20-ounce soda contains 15 teaspoons of sugar, all of it high fructose corn syrup.

Source: https://draxe.com/high-fructose-corn-syrup-dangers/

So many doctors are now beginning to see the light especially if they do research on food additives. Obviously, what you eat is extremely important to your health and wellness. If you are consuming any high fructose corn syrup, you must eliminate it from your diet immediately. Believe me that will not be easy.

DIABETIC PRE – SUPPRESSION STARTER

I think we can all agree that we discovered the main culprit in why any of us are suffering from diabetes. *A toxic body!* So, what exactly have people done to suppress their own diabetes? Are people having success and how are they going about it?

Detoxification is our next step, and I'm going to show you exactly how to do it by drinking a series of handmade tonics from a variety of natural and organic products that are available over-the-counter. I'm referring to super foods, herbs and a combined liquid tincture that you will be able to consume (drink).

The rest of the main detoxification process is 100% contingent on your success. You must be absolutely sugar-free for at least 30 days because:

- ✓ This begins the entire detoxification process.

- ✓ This will allow your body to purge high levels of sugar and drastically drop your A1C.

- ✓ Sugar is the driving force behind elevated glucose levels so the first and fastest way to regain your health is to stop consuming it!

✓ The breakdown of toxins will slowly begin to detoxify your cells

THE DETOXIFICATION STEPS

Here I want to review the full series of steps necessary for:

✓ Pre-detoxification.

✓ Primary detoxification.

✓ Maintenance detoxification.

The steps on the following page will direct you through all of these important phases so that your body is completely clean and free of most inhibiting toxins.

The detoxification process will allow you to overlap

successive steps that are progressive and gentle your body. You will build upon one level of detoxification after another.

When you have completed all the steps we will then discuss how to further push the envelope for diabetic disease suppression.

The human body has amazing potential to heal itself once the right elements are in place and the toxins are removed from your body. After a through detoxification, we will discuss how it is possible to jumpstart your pancreas and other organs.

STEP 1 – REAL WATER

Step 1: Drink ONLY purified water or created water via filtration throughout your day, as well as the purest form of Japanese green longleaf NATURAL / ORGANIC teas for your beverages.

1. **Drinking the cleanest and best form of water** possible is something that we have already discussed. You must not drink any form of municipal city water, or water from wells near farms unless filtered with a Berkey water filter. We suggest the Berkey brand because it is one of the few filtration systems that can remove fluoride and glyphosates from water (as well as numerous other contaminants). Do not proceed to the other steps until you are

capable of producing the cleanest possible water that is as close to 100% toxin free as possible.

2. **Begin drinking water early in the morning when you first wake up on an empty stomach -** there are numerous studies that are emerging that show drinking clean water first thing in the morning *triggers toxins to flow out of your body*. However, this will **not** work with any type of contaminated water.

3. **Increase the amount of water that you consume until you are drinking water throughout the day -** You are attempting to flood your body with clean water and begin to push toxins out of your cells and body; so you must drink large amounts of water. Make sure that you spread the amount of water that you drink throughout the day. For example, you may wish to drink 12 ounce glasses of pure clean drinking water every 2 hours or more often if the environment is really hot.

This process begins the detoxification flush of your body. Think of it like flushing a radiator in a car. Over the period of several weeks this process will significantly help with detoxification and should be something that everyone is doing.

STEP 2 –APPLE CIDER VINEGAR

Step 2: Consume 1 tablespoon of organic apple cider vinegar daily, ½ tablespoon in the morning and ½ tablespoon at night. Apple cider vinegar may be one of the best natural and organic detoxification products on the market. It has dozens of beneficial effects:

- Apple cider vinegar gently detoxifies your body from heavy metals, foodborne toxins and other contaminants in the body.

- Apple cider vinegar can help you control high blood pressure.

- Apple cider vinegar can help you control your weight.

- Apple cider vinegar will help you maintain a natural alkalinity state.

- Apple cider vinegar will help you to regulate your blood sugar.

- Apple cider vinegar improves overall heart health.

- Apple cider vinegar can greatly reduce or eliminate Candida / fungus infections in the body.

- Apple cider vinegar reduces and controls

many digestive ailments.

- Apple cider vinegar can help prevent osteoporosis.

- Apple cider vinegar greatly reduces free radical damage.

Apple cider vinegar is essentially one of the best "curatives" that you could consume on a daily basis.

Simply add half a tablespoon to 8 to 12 ounces crystal clean slightly warm water and drink it on an empty stomach in the morning and just before you go to bed at night.

Do so daily and watch your health begin to improve.

There are many other benefits of Apple cider vinegar, so make sure you do your research and always drink Apple cider vinegar directly mixed in water and never straight from the bottle as this can constrict your esophagus and throat and cause discomfort.

STEP 3 – DETOXIFY YOUR GUT

Step 3: A complete detoxification of your gut - by using one of the best products currently on the market called <u>Oxy Powder</u>.

After careful consideration of multiple products that exist, **Oxy Powder** may be the single best way to completely detoxify your gut.

If you have already been using Apple cider vinegar, you've begun this process. Oxy powder uses *oxygenation of the large and small intestine* to loosen toxins gently and naturally and then pass them out in waste.

Many other forms of gut detoxification products that are sold in stores **can have harsh side effects** and may even keep you from your daily tasks during this process.

Oxy Powder has some of the top reviews in the world and gently cleans your intestines and allows you to void (poop) all of the toxins out of your body when you visit the bathroom.

While using Oxy Powder, you can literally drop between 3 and 7 pounds of some of the most toxic waste that is been clinging to the insides of your intestines for years. You will not need to take time off from work, as long as you can make it to the bathroom several times a day! I have used this product and results were incredible.

It is well worth detoxifying your gut because this is where most health issues begin and then spread to other parts of the body. If you have a clean gut, you are much less likely to develop serious diseases and your immune system greatly improves, as well as your ability to digest nutrients.

Detoxification of your gut should be followed by an introduction of natural healthy gut bacteria, with which Apple cider vinegar also will assist. Start eating Greek yogurt, and other fermented foods to restore natural and good gut bacteria after you are done fixing your gut.

STEP 4 – GET THE BEST POSSIBLE VITAMINS

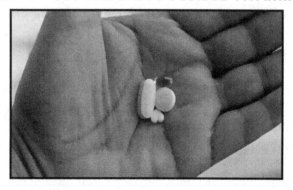

Step four: Obtain the very best possible nutraceuticals and/or vitamins that money can buy.

Part of the reason why people become diabetics is not only due to toxic overload but also because they lack critical vitamins like magnesium. Many studies have demonstrated that high quality, natural and plant based vitamins can have a dramatic impact on the reduction and/or suppression of diabetes.

I'm not talking about synthetic vitamins that anyone can buy over the counter. I am talking about vitamins that have been specifically created from plant extracts and that are 100% natural.

For example, the top vitamin company called Youngevity https://youngevity.com/ might produce some of the world's best natural supplements.

As a diabetic, it is imperative that you have proper vitamins because your body is deficient and needs these additional vitamins to effect repairs and to change the course of the disease in your body. There is simply no way to eat enough healthy food to get the benefits that you need in order to improve your health.

NOW START THE FULL SUPPRESSION PROCESS

Now that you've completed all of the detoxification processes, it's time for the suppression of your diabetes. This will completely cleanse the rest of your body, your kidneys, your pancreas, and even your liver will benefit.

The suppression process works by involving natural and organic substances that overlap each other and have a synergistic effect when it comes to jumpstarting your body and continuing to completely detoxify any remaining toxins that are preventing your body from operating correctly.

Detoxification is a process that should be ongoing, continuous and progressive. The cleaner your body is, the more efficiently it will operate. Even if you are elderly, keeping your organs clean and operating at peak efficiency can allow you to add multiple years to your life.

New research is concluding that if you can remain disease free you will be able to extend your life almost indefinitely! I'm sure you've heard stories of people living to be well past hundred years old, and you could be one of them.

Scientists have discovered that there really is no reason for us to age except when our cells break down and we eventually die if we cannot maintain healthy bodies.

Additional research is beginning to expose the importance of consuming high levels of organic material on a daily basis to extend life and prevent disease. Diabetes is a disease caused by toxic overload so the more we focus on the removing of toxins and the proper functioning of organs, the easier it will be to suppress the disease.

FULL SUPPRESSION OF DIABETES TONIC

Now that you have taken all of the steps for the pre-detoxification, it is time to move into primary detoxification.

Not only is this tonic great for your overall health, but over time you will actually grow to enjoy drinking the tonic. Essentially what the tonic will do is finish the work that was started with your pre-detoxification, which includes the following benefits:

✓ All of the benefits of Apple cider vinegar as mentioned earlier.

✓ A significant reduction of inflammation in your body, which reduces the chance of developing serious diseases.

✓ A complete detoxification of your liver, gallbladder and pancreas. These three organs work together synergistically in order to protect your body from disease.

✓ Significant improvements to digestion, hair and skin.

Here is the suggested mixture and it should be consumed each morning on an empty stomach just like the three detoxification steps. Again, it is critical that you use the cleanest possible water and 100% organic ingredients:

✓ 12 ounces of filtered warm water

✓ 1 tablespoon of raw organic liquid coconut oil

✓ ½ tablespoon of organic apple cider vinegar

✓ 1 tablespoon of organic lime juice

✓ 1 tablespoon of organic lemon juice

✓ One * pinch of Turmeric (organic / ground)

-As mentioned before, everything must be absolutely fresh!

Directions: in a cup place 12 ounces of super filtered, completely toxin free water. Squeeze half an organic line and half an organic lemon and add the juice to 12 ounces of water. Mix in turmeric (about half a teaspoon), coconut oil and stir the entire mixture.

It is important that you mix into water all the ingredients thoroughly, especially the Apple cider vinegar which never be consumed without water.

You should also make sure that you can purchase the cleanest form of turmeric which was processed here in America and not from overseas sources unless the turmeric is considered 100% pure. This is important as some forms of turmeric are polluted with small trace amounts of lead. Processing needs to be organic and natural.

MAINTENANCE TONIC . . .

After finalizing the first two stages, you can now move on to the maintenance detoxification tonic. This is slightly different because you only need to take it every other day.

The tonic now adds rosemary (a small amount), which is a super antioxidant, memory booster, and has dozens of additional health benefits. Simply adding ½ teaspoon of finely ground organic rosemary will do the trick and extend the detoxification tonic without the need to drink it every day, a real bonus when you are traveling or can't always drink the tonic:

Maintenance Tonic:

- ✓ 12 ounces of filtered warm water

- ✓ 1 tablespoon of raw organic liquid coconut

oil

✓ **½ teaspoon organic, finely ground rosemary**

✓ ½ tablespoon of organic apple cider vinegar

✓ 1 tablespoon of organic lime juice

✓ 1 tablespoon of organic lemon juice

✓ One * pinch of Turmeric (organic / ground)

The maintenance tonic is prepared the exact same way as the main detoxification tonic. Do NOT take more than ½ a teaspoon of rosemary (a pinch) as too much can upset your stomach. One half a teaspoon seems to be enough for all the health benefits.

AT A GLANCE STEPS & TIMEFRAME FOR IT ALL

Here we are going to lay out the exact timeframe, steps and functions of the entire process to help with full understanding:

Diabetic Suppression– The suppression starter steps are the *detoxification steps* as mentioned earlier in the guide that fall under the "pre-detoxification" label:

➢ **Pre-detoxification** - Here you follow the

first 4 steps that lead into the primary detoxification:

➢ **Step 1 – Real Water** – start creating and drinking over the course of the entire program.

➢ **Step 2 –Apple Cider Vinegar**– Start drinking over the course of the entire program.

➢ **Step 3 – Detoxify Your Gut** – 3-5 days, repeat twice for the first month.

➢ **Step 4 – Get The Best Possible Vitamins** – start taking the vitamins over the course of the entire program.

➢ **Primary detoxification** – take the main detoxification tonic for at least 30 days before switching to the maintenance tonic.

➢ **Maintenance detoxification** – switch to the maintenance tonic and drink it every other day. After 30 days, drink it every third day.

That's it! These steps are easy to follow. Simply start at the top and work your way down. Make sure that if you start having increases in blood sugar that you go back to the maintenance tonic every other day if switching to every third say has diminishing returns.

SHOPPING LIST FOR EVERYTHING YOU NEED

✓ **Distilled / filtered water** with NO additives of any kind OR

✓ **Berkey water filter** to make clean water from filtration.

✓ **One bottle of organic apple cider vinegar** (Braggs is the best with organic white sediment on the bottom).

✓ **Vitamins from a top proven plant extract based source** and do NOT buy over the counter crap from places like GNC (NO synthetic GMO laced products).

✓ **Organic limes** (do NOT use the processed plastic filled limes).

✓ **Organic lemons** (do NOT use the processed plastic filled lemons).

✓ **Organic coconut oil** (100% natural, virgin and liquid form).

✓ **Organic finely ground Turmeric**.

✓ **Organic and finely ground rosemary**.

When you are shopping, try to get all of your ingredients from health food stores or farmer's markets if possible. Check to make sure everything is toxin free, unprocessed and natural.

You should also locate good sources of organic foods so that you can continue to improve your health and reset your body.

Always make sure you have several clean sources for organic produce.

OTHER CONSIDERATIONS

- **Do NOT consume ANY processed sugar for at least 30 days** and significantly longer if possible. Start weaning yourself off of as much sugar as possible except natural / local honey.

- **Once your body is restored,** you will be able to eat small amounts, but always think of sugar like rat poison if you are a diabetic. Consuming as little as possible when detoxifying your body is very important.

- **ONLY use Stevia while detoxifying -** Stevia is much better than sugar as it is a plant extract. I carry a small bottle with me everywhere I go and use small amounts of it for coffee, teas etc. Find out more here:

- http://www.livescience.com/39601 -stevia-facts-safety.html

- **The detoxification steps** will work in conjunction with your body. The steps are designed to complement and overlay a progressive series of cleansing actions. By following the steps, you will not shock your system or need to stop the process.

- **Watch blood sugar like a hawk–** You MUST carefully track your blood sugar especially during the entire process so that you can gradually wean yourself off of your diabetic meds. You should keep a journal and use it to show your doctor and explain what you are doing. The readings will prove to the doctor you are on the right course.

- **Reduce medication over time based on blood sugar readings at least 5 times a day** – as your blood sugar continues to drop to normal levels you MUST wean yourself off of meds. Do NOT attempt this without your doctor. You do NOT want to have your blood sugar so low that you go into a coma.

- **Start eating super foods** for snacks. This can include blueberries, strawberries, nuts of all kinds (unsalted & skin intact), avocados, and lose leaf teas of all kinds (natural and unprocessed).

- **Soak in a hot bath daily or long hot shower** – There are many reasons to do this as a diabetic. Hot water has been the secret to longevity for people in Japan, and many studies are emerging on the benefits of daily hot water immersion.

- **Intermittent fasting** – Exciting new research is happening in this field. Intermittent fasting was part of our lifestyle as hunter/gathers for over a million (possibly longer) years or so. Our genetics cause us to NEED fasting and studies are showing that fasting up to 72 hours may completely reset our endocrine system, and heal damage in your body thought un-healable (i.e. wounds, nerves, brain cells etc.). Some diabetics are claiming that ongoing intermittent fasting "reversed" their diabetes when they resumed an organic diet after fasting. Check with your doctor, as this might not be advisable for your current condition.

- **Lose extra weight through intermittent fasting & diet change** – This should make sense. Here you start a good organic diet that is mostly plant based. Skip eating twice a week for 24 hours at least and start a low impact exercise regimen like beginner's yoga (also very good for diabetics).

- **If man made it, don't eat it** – a very simple rule to follow. If you do, your health will change for the better quickly. Stick to super foods, organic produce and grass fed, free range, no hormone meats. NEVER buy your meat from big chains (i.e. Wal-Mart) as much of their foods are tainted with toxins. Remember China now handles most of our food processing production and they have been caught doing horrible things to all foods.

Read more here:

https://offgridsurvival.com/foodsupplycontrol/

RESTORING HEALTH IS A PROCESS

Restoring health has always been a process. You do not become unhealthy overnight (usually) and steps leading up to a serious illness can be almost always prevented.

In this section we're going to discuss several ways that restoring health can be done systematically and progressively.

Unlike fad diets, quick fixes and snake oil products, here you have the opportunity to completely restore your health by relearning **what** you eat, **how** you eat and even **when** you eat.

It should make complete sense to you that something we do to our bodies **multiple times a day** (what you eat) has a dramatic impact on your overall health. The food that you take into your body must be the cleanest source possible and we have been discussing this all throughout the guide.

I want you to take the next several pages into serious consideration!

HOW TO CHANGE YOUR DIET EASILY

Unlike ridiculous fad diets, or starvation diets (this is not intermittent fasting!) Your goal is to provide your body with the proper nutrients and fuel so that it can function right and completely fight off diabetes.

One of the best ways to do this is to plan in advance how you can begin to change the number of times you are eating non-organic foods. Most people eat between four and eight times a day. We've been brought up to have breakfast, lunch, dinner and snacks.

Is this really a healthy way to eat? Absolutely not! By simply comparing our genetic memories with our ancient ancestors, let's take a look at how they typically ate food:

Breakfast - breakfast for our ancestors often consisted of berries, nuts, grains, tubers and anything else that could be harvested quickly.

Lunch – Hunter / gatherers typically did not stop for lunch and would use available daylight hours to continue to gather different types of foods to bring back to the tribe. Anything that could be found along the way may have been used for a quick snack.

Dinner -primitive man would seek out high calorie kills and bring it back to the tribe. Unfortunately, this did not happen daily and it was quite possible for people to go several days without eating large amounts of calories from protein, bone broth and marrow.

We have discovered that when we mimic the same type of hunter/ gatherer lifestyle, this induces extreme health and wellness, especially if this type of eating is coupled with occasional intense exercise.

Exercise should start out easy but become challenging.

When you compare this with the typical sedentary lifestyle of people today, is it any wonder that we are so unhealthy?

The human body was never intended to consume large quantities of sugar and doing so is equivalent to introducing a dangerous poison into your body. The typical food intake of primitive man may look something like this:

Day one – a handful of berries in the morning.

Water to drink. Field greens for the afternoon and evening.

Day two – a small amount of honey followed by rabbit stew with lentils, tubers and herbs.

Day three – here the tribe has managed to get a large calorie kill so now we can add protein and high fat intake to their diet along with field greens and tubers.

Day four – the tribe is on the move today so they will only be drinking water and eating a handful of fruits and berries.

Day five - an intense storm keeps the tribe huddled in their shelters. Nobody eats today.

Day six - the tribe emerges after the storms and begins traveling to follow game. Hunters are out looking for food.

Day seven – the tribe manages another high calorie proteins kill but nobody gets to eat until later in the evening.

As you can see, primitive man ate very little, was constantly on the move and was periodically experiencing intermittent fasting. Human beings thrived on this diet and it is the modern foundation to what professionals are now calling the Paleo diet. We should be mimicking this lifestyle because we are genetically programmed to become healthy if we do so!

CONSIDER PRIMITIVE EATING TO REVERSE DIABETES

If you haven't already figured it out, primitive eating may be the best possible solution along with the steps in this guide.

You should follow all of the steps first, and as your health improves, systematically switch over to primitive eating. The goal is to follow this type of diet and/or lifestyle at least 80% of the time.

By doing so, you will guarantee that your body will continue to grow in overall fitness and health. You will use food as your primary medicine, and so you need not worry about side effects from drugs.

Ask any diabetic if that sounds like a wonderful deal, and they will tell you "absolutely." The good thing about eating primitive foods that you **do not have to be overly concerned about blood sugar**; very few super foods and or whole foods will seriously spike your blood sugar as long as they are low glycemic and you eat in moderation.

Low glycemic foods are helpful if they are whole foods and 100% natural. Never buy processed low glycemic diet foods, as yet again they are filled with toxins.

Also, you should consider going from the current

diet you were eating to a primitive diet over time. You should never completely quit cold turkey the food you are eating, but rather slowly and gradually replace high calorie, high carbohydrate processed foods for the better food choices.

Finally, if you have any doubts as to whether or not primitive eating is good for you, tens of thousands of people have switched to this type of lifestyle and many of them are reporting vibrant health, increased physical strength and stamina and other health benefits that are essentially too numerous to list here. Maybe it's time for you to consider primitive eating to reverse your diabetes.

WHAT TO EXPECT IN 90 DAYS ON THIS PROGRAM

Once you have followed all the steps in this guide, you should begin to see blood sugar readings drop considerably.

You will also experience other physiological and even psychological changes; so I wanted to make a list of these for you so that you are not surprised and can anticipate what will happen to you:

> **Consistent and downward blood glucose readings** from high to manageable (i.e. 250 to 190). Remember it takes time for your body to heal, so the reduction will be gradual will also be based on the kind of diet you are eating.

➤ **Greatly reduced cravings for sugar -** essentially sugar to a diabetic is like crack cocaine to a drug abuser. By completely weaning yourself off of processed sugars, you will notice that you will begin to feel better almost immediately and that over time, cravings will gradually lessen.

➤ **Improve mental clarity and focus -** When you're eating the correct foods, mind and body begin to work well together. A mental fog that follows most diabetics begins to lift and you will notice being able to think more clearly and make better decisions.

➤ **A gradual reduction to possible complete elimination of all diabetic drugs -** The idea is to gradually wean yourself off of these drugs as well because they are only maintaining your disease and not curing it.

➤ **Improved skin tone, shiny hair, bright eyes** – additional awesome benefits of following all the steps in this guide.

➤ **A vibrant look of health and wellness -** as your health continues to prove, and your body is finally working correctly, you will begin to exude health and have a general appearance of someone who is radiant and well.

➤ **Weight loss without dieting -** By following all the steps in this guide you'll naturally lose weight because you'll be eating the correct foods. Some people become concerned because you will tend to drop a significant amount of weight; but this is natural and is a form of detoxification in and of itself.

➤ **Reduced depression -** Eating the correct balance of nutrients is more effective than any prescription drug for depression. When you're getting the correct balance of nutrients your mind is in balance with your body.

➤ **Improved sleeping patterns -** Eating the right food and keeping your diabetes suppressed means that we are able to have much more productive sleep, which will continue to improve our health as well. Diabetics need at least eight hours of uninterrupted sleep and good sleeping patterns.

➤ **Improved digestion -** A majority of digestive issues, such as Crohn's disease, are caused by eating junk foods. Switching to whole foods and primitive eating can cure all digestive issues over time because your body has time to heal and regenerate.

➢ **Stable and easily maintained blood sugar levels** – the result of all of this for a diabetic is near normal blood sugar levels.

These are all fantastic reasons why following the steps in this guide can truly benefit you.

Now you completely understand how to repair almost all damage to your body, by simply following primitive eating.

HOW IT ALL WORKED FOR "RALPH"

One man by the name of **Ralph** was following the advice in this guide. He informed his doctor that he was attempting to utilize natural methods to help control his blood sugar.

I wanted to include Ralph's story because he was a typical person who was diabetic and he is proof that this system works.

Ralph lived in Upstate New York and was a father of two boys. About ten years ago he began to notice he felt tired and lethargic. Over time, it was discovered that he was having issues controlling his blood sugar.

Like most people, we listen to our doctor at first. When Ralph visited his physician, he was told that according to the blood tests, he was most likely pre -diabetic.

As you recall from earlier parts of the guide, we explain what happens to people when they first receive their diagnosis and Ralph was no different.

Ralph began taking prescription drugs, which were supposed to regulate his blood sugar and help him. This principal medication was Metformin. Unknown to Ralph, side effects of this prescription drug include constipation, diarrhea, headaches, dizziness and of course reduced blood sugar.

It's interesting to note that the drug also reduces the level of vitamin B12 in the body, which is a critical nutrient. It is absolutely necessary for the health and well-being of all people, especially diabetics!

While his diabetic symptoms began to subside, he noticed that after about a year on prescription drugs that his diabetes was actually getting worse and he needed more medication to achieve the same maintenance results.

Ralph hated being on the medication but he figured he had no choice and this was just something he had to endure.

After Ralph's second year of being a diabetic he began to notice that he was having issues with his kidneys and pancreas. It was at this point that the doctor suggested adding insulin, because it would be easier for Ralph to control (maintain) this disease.

It was at this point that Ralph started taking regular shots of insulin in order to further control his diabetes, which was slowly becoming uncontrollable. Even with insulin, Ralph would occasionally have high blood sugar glucose readings, sometimes as high as 400 . . .

Of course, the insulin would always reduce his blood sugar to manageable levels, but what was really happening in his body **was that all of his organs were beginning to shut down.**

While insulin is a godsend to people and can extend their lives, it actually teaches your body not to function properly. Because of this, Ralph began searching the Internet for people who claimed that it was possible to at least control if not outright repress their own diabetes.

Ralph discovered this guide and began to apply its teachings.

At first it was difficult for Ralph, but he began to realize that diabetes was not necessarily his fault, and that all the food he believed was edible was actually filled with toxins; the primary reason why Ralph contracted diabetes in the first place.

Ralph began to follow the steps to detoxify his body so that it would begin to function normally. He stayed on all of the detoxification tonics and over a period of approximately 60 days, he saw his blood sugar finally improve dramatically.

Ralph then switched to eating almost purely organic foods, and over a period of another 30 days, saw dramatic increases in his overall health and wellness.

Ralph was very excited by the results because he was slowly reducing his medication while increasing primitive eating and using the steps in this guide to detoxify his body. What was truly amazing about the entire process is that it was actually cheaper for Ralph to follow the steps in this guide than to maintain his diabetes using expensive drugs that had horrible side effects and were not healing his body.

Ralph began to increase exercise once he regained some of his strength. First, he started out with yoga because it was very low impact and he could do this exercise at his own pace.

Ralph became quite the expert and when combining meditation and breathing exercises, his stress greatly reduced which also benefited his health. Ralph began to see real improvements and his stamina increased exponentially.

Once Ralph added intermittent fasting and primitive eating, his body was completely healed, and even though doctors say can never cure diabetes, he proved them all wrong.

Ralph reverses diabetes and so can you.

The steps in this guide are not difficult to do, are not expensive and have a huge track record of success helping and healing diabetics. What do you have to lose except the disease? And that is something all of us are very grateful to do.

HOW TO CONVINCE YOUR DOCTOR TO WORK WITH YOU

This is one of the last sections in this e-book, but one of the most important. I would like to give you some basic background information about doctors and why it isn't working to try and find the right type of doctor who will work with you while you are going through this process.

The first thing you need to know is that doctors today do not receive the same kind of training they did years ago. Nutrition is barely discussed nor are alternative healing methods.

The pharmaceutical companies make hundreds of billions of dollars off of diabetes so they are protecting their cash cow. They do so by **suppressing research**, publishing misleading information and funding most of the training that doctors receive today.

The typical doctor who goes to med school has almost all of their expenses supported by large pharmaceutical companies, who incidentally are creating and writing a fair amount of the coursework the doctors are receiving. It is all about writing prescriptions now.

Since **ongoing education is also required** to continue to practice medicine, pharmaceutical companies hold paid training for many doctors in exotic places. Most doctors simply need to sign an attendance sheet and then go enjoy a five star hotel and scenic places where many of these conferences are held.

The ongoing education consists of a variety of drugs that can be used and the latest drugs that will be coming on the market. Many doctors receive financial incentives not only to promote the drugs, but to actually prescribe them even if they are clueless as to what is really capable of doing to the human body.

The bottom line is simple: the drug companies control our doctors by providing them many of the benefits that they already should be receiving for being a good doctor.

Another huge consideration is that the primary training the doctors receive is simply inadequate and has nothing to do with curing disease or holistic medicine.

Yet we've seen the results of holistic medicine, and it is quite capable of providing different levels of disease repression or in some cases out right curatives.

By understanding all of this information, you realize that doctors are essentially "drug pushers" unless they happen to fall outside of the typical norm. For example, holistic doctors study natural ways to heal the human body and are very much interested in natural ways to do so.

You should also consider that your doctor may know absolutely nothing about the origins of diabetes. Typically, most doctors will blame diabetes **on the person who has it;** but as you can see, many of us can contract diabetes simply by interacting with our environment.

While all of us are required to eat healthy in order to stay healthy, it simply is ludicrous to blame the diabetic when there are so many smoking guns for diabetes that have been linked to a toxic environment.

With all of this understood, now you have a new way to think about how to approach your doctor. The very first step may be to find the correct doctor in the first place!

For example, remember Ralph? His doctor only wanted to prescribe medications for him and didn't want to hear anything about a so-called "folk cure." The doctor even warned Ralph not to attempt this as he might injure his health further. This is exactly what doctors are taught and why you must consider finding one that does NOT follow this thinking.

Yes, there are a large number of highly qualified doctors that may know exactly what you're attempting to do because they focus their practice on holistic medicine.

So, the best way to involve your doctor in the first place is to consider finding the right doctor who will listen to what you have to say and already practices most of what you're trying to do.

Here is what I suggest you do to find the closest holistic doctor who will support what you want to do with your health:

> ➢ **Look online for a doctor who believes in holistic medicine** and working with patients who want to take advantage of it.

> ➢ **Find other diabetics who are like-minded** and ask them about how they handled their doctor.

> ➢ **Invest in a good journal and track your blood sugar** and foods you eat. This is valuable empirical information for any doctor and can prove that what you are doing works.

> ➢ **Never go to a general practitioner** unless you can see their track record of treating diabetes.

Follow all the latest research as several breakthroughs are about to happen. For example, India has recently claimed they have a new shot that eliminates diabetes.

Read more here:

http://timesofindia.indiatimes.com/home/science/
Type-1-diabetes-cure-within-reach-after-
breakthrough-that-could-spell-end-of-insulin-
injections-for-millions/articleshow/44774870.cms

- ➢ **Show your doctor your progress** in your journal as this helps convince him or her that you know what you are talking about.

- ➢ **Ask about any complications** with medication. Typically there are not any, but always ask.

Many doctors are also willing to listen to you because their main job is to be like a detective; what works to make you better usually will be supported by most doctors, as long as you can prove you are getting better.

Always remember that a doctor's primary concern is the ability for them to generate sufficient income to keep their practice doors open. Due to the high cost of medical malpractice and other expenses, most doctors are willing to sell their ideals in exchange for regular income, the kind that comes with writing prescriptions all the time.

The only person that's truly going to be 100% in favor of everything you do to improve your health will be *you*. Most doctors are motivated by money, power and prestige.

Even though most people get into medicine for all the right reasons, anyone that has worked in the field will tell you that it is very corrupt and its focus is not always the patient's best interests. Doctors are routinely paid for delivering vaccines and prescriptions especially with the latest drugs they're constantly being flooded on the market.

We've seen the results of bad drugs, and as long as there are doctors pushing these drugs on unsuspecting hapless victims, medicine is no longer going to be primarily about curing anyone.

That's what happened to medicine today thanks to greedy politicians, greedy drug companies and everyone else in between who makes 'a cut' off of your poor health.

Find the right doctor in the first place if at all possible!

FIND SUPPORT GROUPS

One of the final bits of information I wish to offer to you is to consider finding the very best support groups out there.

If you can't find a support group, maybe you should start one in your area. Support groups can do many things to help everyone benefit:

✓ **Friends** - People who are going through the exact same thing you are may have found creative ways to deal with the disease that can help you too. You will make good friends and you may be able to help each other when diabetes becomes too much to handle by yourself.

✓ **Support** - Not only can you make good friends, but the main purpose of this support group is to assist you in dealing with whatever issue that group is about. There may be information that you are unaware of that could completely change the situation for you for the better. Being able to meet with other people who suffer from the same disease means that you can exchange notes and ideas on how to make yourself better.

✓ **Networking** - Another bonus of being part of a support group is that many different types of helpful solutions may be readily available and proven to work by other members. If one member has discovered something that makes their life easier, they can share this information with everybody else. Networking is always a benefit of joining any support group.

✓ **Exercise and activities** - Diabetics know they must exercise to maintain health and what a fun way to do it -- with other people whom also understand this mandate. It is far better to join in with like-minded people than to try to exercise on your own with people that are not diabetic. You will not only enjoy the group activity but you get much needed exercise.

✓ **Financial support** - Many support groups have funding and grants from businesses, entrepreneurs and philanthropists. There is money available to help you when you really need it, especially if you're a contributing member of the group on a regular basis.

✓ **Adult daycare / sitting services** - Support groups also offer ways to help others who are going through a difficult time. For example, as a new member you might be required twice a month to make yourself available for eight hours so that you can do chores, help other adults that are suffering as well as share the load when it comes to disease management.

✓ **Innovation, new research and testing** - Support groups also offer the ability to be involved in the latest diabetic research and testing of new products. While nobody likes being a guinea pig, you might just stumble across something very useful that truly improves your health and wellness.

✓ **Safety and security** – Having the ability to network with other people that are suffering with the same disease means that you can count on these people to help you when you have issues pertaining to your safety and security. For example, it is discovered that a particular diabetic medicine is causing premature death, but the information is suppressed. You are much more likely to learn this information and have it revealed to you when many people come together and pool their collective knowledge.

Support groups can also be created by going to https://www.meetup.com/. Millions of people create meet ups and diabetic\s are no exception. This is also a great way to meet like-minded people if you appreciate certain hobbies, events etc.

Why not take the time to create your own group? You could help literally hundreds maybe even thousands of people who are diabetic and that's a whole lot of positive karma coming in your direction. At your next opportunity make sure you either find or create a perfect meet up group.

CONCLUSION AND BEYOND

I wanted to first take the time to say thank you for reading this amazing guide. I have devoted a considerable amount of time to the research as well as finally explaining to people *exactly what diabetes really is* and not just what we are spoon fed from modern medicine and large pharmaceutical companies.

In this guide we discussed many controversial topics like: why hasn't there been a medical cure for diabetes released? We further explain the exact medical definition of what we are told diabetes is *should be* according to modern medicine. Boy, are they wrong!

I reveal a completely different definition of what diabetes is based on **years of research and having been a diabetic**. I explain how toxic overload eventually leads to dysfunction in the body and *smoldering illnesses* such as diabetes, which are caused by out-of-control inflammation by toxins.

I next go into exactly what junk food does to you. This includes all of the other forms of toxins that we are absorbing on a daily basis.

Most people are not aware of this.

In addition, I go into detail about the real truth and the numerous lies and disinformation that exist about the disease, which most people believe, but are untrue.

I also discussed exactly what diabetes type I and type II are as well as good information on controlling the disease.

Next, I discussed some of the better ways of diabetic management and *some of the latest diabetic research details*.

I also discussed diabetes from another perspective and how it is possible *to begin suppression of the disease* by changing what you eat and utilizing organic herbs and super foods in combination to completely suppress the disease over time.

Also, I lay out exact steps and give you several recipes for diabetic suppression tinctures that you can drink on a regular basis which are cheap, healthy, have no side effects and are easy to make.

I also explain what to do *in the maintenance stage* after you have your disease under control so that it never comes back.

Finally, I give you detailed information including 'at a glance' steps and timelines bringing everything together on a single page; so that you completely understand how the process should be followed.

Next, I explore the process of restoring your health and how you can change your diet progressively over time so that it is not a system shock when you start changing foods and eating really healthy.

I also talk about **_primitive eating_** and how this will affect you and your health over the next 90 days.

Finally, I bring everything together with a story about **_Ralph_** and the best steps for convincing your doctor to work with you. This includes finding support groups and we've explained exactly how you can do just that, even if you want to be the one who starts the support group.

I have distilled literally years of information on how to reverse diabetes based on solid research, evidence, proof and direct information that you can immediately begin to use to reverse your own diabetes.

All the information is now at your fingertips and all you have to do to systematically, gently and effectively reduce your diabetes is to follow the steps.

Now you have the solution you've been looking for and all you have to do is use this guide.

I'd like to take the opportunity to say thank you and congratulate you from the bottom of my heart for finishing this book. The next step is to implement what you have learned.

11 SUPER HERBS & SPICES That WILL POSITIVELY IMPACT YOUR BLOOD SUGAR LEVELS!

Get The **CLINICALLY PROVEN & ALL NATURAL HERBS/ SPICES** that Will Allow You To Finally REVERSE Your DIABETES (with no Medications, Exercises, or Dieting, and do it in as little as a few short weeks!)

Get This Free Book Here

http://bit.ly/DiabetesSuperHerbs

(Url is Case Sensitive)